BRIGHT IDEA BOOKS

Lakes
IN THE Ocean
AND OTHER COOL
UNDERWATER
FACTS

by Kimberly M. Hutmacher

Content Consultant

Hans G. Dam, PhD
Professor of Marine Sciences
University of Connecticut

CAPSTONE PRESS
a capstone imprint

Bright Idea Books are published by Capstone Press
1710 Roe Crest Drive, North Mankato, Minnesota 56003
www.mycapstone.com

Library of Congress Cataloging-in-Publication Data
Names: Hutmacher, Kimberly, author.
Title: Lakes in the ocean and other cool underwater facts / by Kimberly M. Hutmacher.
Description: North Mankato, Minnesota : Capstone Press, 2019. | Series: Mind
   blowing science facts | Includes bibliographical references and index. |
   Audience: Age 9-12. | Audience: Grade 4 to 6.
Identifiers: LCCN 2018035982 | ISBN 9781543557671 (hardcover : alk. paper) |
   ISBN 9781543557992 (ebook)
Subjects: LCSH: Submarine topography--Juvenile literature. | Marine ecology--Juvenile literature.
Classification: LCC GC83 .H88 2019 | DDC 551.46/83--dc23
LC record available at https://lccn.loc.gov/2018035982

Editorial Credits
Editor: Meg Gaertner
Designer: Becky Daum
Production Specialist: Colleen McLaren

Photo Credits
iStockphoto: baona, 5, beusbeus, 21, Eric Broder Van Dyke, 23, rightdx, 25, 28, RyanJLane, 24–25;
NASA: JPL, 7; NOAA: Gavin Eppard, WHOI/Expedition to the Deep Slope/OER, 14–15, IFE, URI–IAO,
UW, Lost City Science Party/OAR/OER/The Lost City 2005 Expedition, 13, NSF, 17, Pacific Ring
of Fire 2004 Expedition/NOAA Office of Ocean Exploration/Dr. Bob Embley, NOAA PMEL, Chief
Scientist, 18–19, Rhode Island Institute for Archaeological Oceanography/Secrets of the Gulf
Expedition/NOS/NMS/FGBNMS, 8–9; Shutterstock Images: Alexeysun, 30–31, Ethan Daniels, 27,
Khoroshunova Olga, 10, Neil Bromhall, 26, SNT4, cover, Vadim Petrakov, 11

Printed in the United States of America.
PA48

TABLE OF CONTENTS

AMAZING Underwater World

There are forests in the ocean. There are lakes and waterfalls too. Some ocean fish light up. Others have no faces. The ocean is amazing!

Many deep-sea creatures give off their own light.

WILD
Water

Ocean covers 71 percent of Earth. It has an average depth of 12,400 feet (3,780 meters). Visible light cannot pass below 330 feet (100 m). The ocean is pitch black below that level.

Images from space show how much of Earth is covered by water.

An underwater lake formed
in the Gulf of Mexico,
off the coast of Texas.

LAKES IN THE OCEAN

Rock and salt form the ocean floor. There is water beneath the floor. Sometimes the water seeps up through the salt. It **dissolves** the salt. The ocean floor sinks. The salt water fills the space left behind. This water is saltier than ocean water. It is very **dense**. It does not mix with the ocean water. Instead, it forms an underwater lake.

UNDERWATER WATERFALL

Some of Earth's waterfalls are underwater. One is in the Denmark Strait. This is between Greenland and Iceland. Cold water is denser than hot water. Cold water sinks. It drops straight down. It forms an ocean waterfall. The water drops about 11,500 feet (3,500 m).

There is an underwater waterfall off the coast of Mauritius, an island nation east of Africa.

Angel Falls is in Venezuela.

RECORD HEIGHTS

The tallest land waterfall is Angel Falls. It is 3,211 feet (979 m) tall. But the Denmark Strait waterfall is three times taller.

CHAPTER 3

IN THE
Depths

The largest mountain range is the Mid-Ocean Ridge. It is 40,400 miles (65,000 kilometers) long. It is underwater. Some of its peaks rise above sea level. It covers almost a quarter of Earth's surface.

A jellyfish swims
by a formation in the
Mid-Atlantic Ridge, part
of the Mid-Ocean Ridge.

CHALLENGER DEEP

The Mariana Trench is in the Pacific Ocean. It is a canyon. The ocean's deepest point is there. This point is called Challenger Deep. It is about 36,070 feet (10,990 m) deep. The **water pressure** is very heavy. It is 1,000 times greater than at sea level. Imagine 50 jumbo jets on top of you. That is what Challenger Deep would feel like.

The *Alvin* has taken three people to an ocean depth of 23,170 feet (7,000 m).

CHAPTER 4

UNDERWATER Fireplaces

Earth's top layer is divided into pieces. They are called **tectonic plates**. Sometimes their movements create volcanoes. Most volcano eruptions happen in the ocean. They happen underwater. **Lava** flows along the ocean floor.

BIRTH OF AN ISLAND

An ocean volcano erupts. The lava cools. It hardens. More layers form over time. The volcano gets bigger. It reaches the ocean's surface. Then it forms an island.

Lava spews as an underwater volcano erupts.

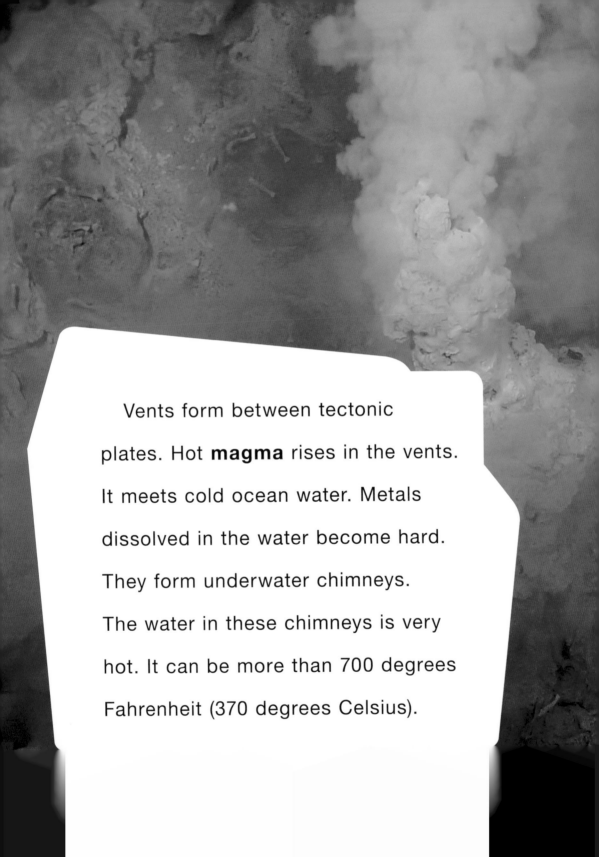

Vents form between tectonic plates. Hot **magma** rises in the vents. It meets cold ocean water. Metals dissolved in the water become hard. They form underwater chimneys. The water in these chimneys is very hot. It can be more than 700 degrees Fahrenheit (370 degrees Celsius).

The water in the chimneys can get twice as hot as the temperature needed to cook a turkey.

CHAPTER 5

OCEAN
Plants

Oceans have forests. Giant kelp is the largest form of seaweed. It grows in forests. It can grow more than 100 feet (30 m) tall. Oceans also have grass. Seagrasses are underwater plants. Their beds can grow large. Some can even be seen from space!

Schools of fish swim
through kelp forests.

ONLY SO DEEP

Plants need sunlight to survive.
Ocean plants only grow so deep.
They live in the top 330 feet (100 m)
of the water. There is not enough
sunlight below that depth.

CHAPTER 6

OCEAN
Animals

Scientists know of more than 200,000 ocean **species**. But they believe there are millions more. More than 80 percent of the ocean is still unexplored.

The blue whale is the largest animal ever. Its heart is the size of a car. Oarfish are the longest fish. They have snakelike bodies. They grow to be 56 feet (17 m) long!

Oarfish usually live in the deep sea. But they sometimes wash up on shore.

An octopus is an amazing animal. It can change color. It can shoot out ink to protect itself. An octopus can squeeze through tiny holes. It can solve problems. It can use tools. Scientists think it can even learn from experience.

Octopus arms are covered in suckers that can grasp objects.

There are more than
300 species of squid
in the world.

The giant squid can grow
to be 33 feet (10 m) long.
It has the largest eyes of all
animals. Each eye is about
the size of a dinner plate.

Anglerfish wait until their prey is in range. Then they attack.

DEEP-SEA CREATURES

Some fish have clear skin. Some glow in the dark. An anglerfish has a built-in fishing pole. A growth on its head gives off light. The light attracts prey.

The frilled shark is a **living fossil**. It has not changed much in millions of years. It looks like a thick eel. A real deep-sea eel has no face. Its mouth pops out to catch food. Then its mouth goes back inside its body.

The hairy frogfish is another ocean creature. Instead of swimming, it walks on its fins.

GLOSSARY

dense
closely compacted and thick

dissolve
to become part of a liquid
such as water

lava
molten rock that forms from
magma that has been cooled

living fossil
an animal that closely
resembles an ancient creature

magma
hot fluid underneath
Earth's surface

species
a group of plants or animals
of the same kind that can
produce offspring together

tectonic plate
a large piece of Earth's top
layer that can move along
Earth's surface

water pressure
the force of the water pushing
down on a certain area

TRIVIA

1. Ocean animals make plenty of noise. But there are other ocean sounds that scientists cannot explain. They could be from icebergs breaking apart. They could be from unknown animals.

2. Coral is a tiny creature. Corals make a sort of skeleton out of their bodies. These skeletons stack over time. They form massive coral reefs. Coral also makes its own sunscreen to protect itself from the sun. Scientists are studying coral to create better sunscreen for people.

3. There are more artifacts on the ocean floor than in all museums combined. These include items from about one million shipwrecks.

ACTIVITY

SALT WATER VS. FRESH WATER

Almost all of Earth's water, including the water in the oceans, is salt water. Learn what happens when salt is added to water through this experiment.

You will need:

1 bunch of grapes

3 tall glasses of water

2 tablespoons of salt

2 tablespoons of sugar

2 tablespoons of cornstarch

1 spoon for stirring

1. Mix the salt into one glass of water. Stir until you can no longer see the salt. Label this glass "salt."

2. Repeat step one for the sugar and the cornstarch. Use the other two glasses of water.

3. Drop a few grapes into each glass. Did the grapes float or sink?

Salt water is denser than fresh water. It sinks underneath objects that are less dense. Many objects that sink in fresh water will float in salt water.

FURTHER RESOURCES

Ready to dive into more amazing ocean facts?
Check out these resources:

NASA Climate Kids: Gallery of Oceans
https://climatekids.nasa.gov/ocean-gallery/

National Geographic Kids: Ocean
https://kids.nationalgeographic.com/explore/nature/habitats/ocean/#coral-reef-
    fish.jpg

Yasuda, Anita. *Oceans and Seas! With 25 Science Projects for Kids*. White River
    Junction, Vt.: Nomad Press, 2018.

Curious about deep-sea creatures? Learn more here:

DK Find Out!: Deep-Sea Fish
www.dkfindout.com/us/animals-and-nature/fish/deep-sea-fish/

DK Find Out!: Umbrella Octopuses
www.dkfindout.com/us/animals-and-nature/octopuses-and-squid/umbrella-
    octopuses/

Lynette, Rachel. *Deep-Sea Anglerfish and Other Fearsome Fish*. Chicago, Ill.:
    Raintree, 2012.

INDEX